FONDLY REMEMBERED

by Gareth Armstrong

SAMUEL FRENCH

samuelfrench.co.uk

FOR AMATEUR PRODUCTION ENQUIRIES

UNITED KINGDOM AND WORLD EXCLUDING NORTH AMERICA

plays@SamuelFrench-London.co.uk

020 7255 4302/01

Each title is subject to availability from Samuel French,

depending upon country of performance.

ABOUT THE AUTHOR

Gareth has combined the roles of actor, director, and writer throughout a career that has taken to him to over fifty countries. He has been a member of the RSC, performed at Shakespeare's Globe and in the West End. He has directed a wide repertoire of work all over the UK as well as in Europe and America. He wrote his own one-man show, *Shylock*, which toured internationally for ten years. Since then he has specialised in creating solo theatre pieces for other performers, and *Wilde Without the Boy*, his dramatisation of Oscar Wilde's *De Profundis*, tours internationally. His other published work includes a memoir, *A Case for Shylock – Around the World with Shakespeare's Jew*, with a foreword by Judi Dench, and an instructional book for actors, *So You Want To Do A Solo Show*. He records audiobooks, video games, has played three different running characters in *The Archers* and is an occasional contributor to the BBC programme *From Our Own Correspondent*.

AUTHOR'S NOTE

There are lots of plays about funerals. Funerals offer plenty of scope for drama. But a Memorial Service, when the emotions are less raw, and people can say what they *really* think, is much more fertile ground for comedy.

This play was written for a particular group of highly talented actors, all of whom had reached pensionable age. They found, as so many seniors do, that although they were still keen to work and had a wealth of experience to offer, the professional opportunities became fewer with age.

It was from a dinner party conversation that the idea of a play written specifically and exclusively for them became a reality. We didn't want it to deal with subjects that normally preoccupy writers dealing with *the third age:* dementia, bereavement, loneliness and death. We wanted it to reflect the reality of shared lives, memories, and the positive things that come with being more mature. Several similar get-togethers yielded a wealth of stories, a mountain of gossip and an almost indecent amount of laughter. All those elements are part of celebrating a life, and theatre should be a celebration of life.

ACKNOWLEDGEMENTS AND THANKS

Roger Llewellyn (rehearsal photos).

Joel Luther-Braun (lighting technician).

Roger Davenport, John Rowe, Holly Wilson, Sandra Duncan, Eunice Roberts, Gary Raymond, Delena Kidd, Timothy Carlton, Wanda Ventham.

The Bedford Park Fesival.

Rev. Kevin Morris.

David Roper and all at Heavy Entertainment.

ORIGINAL PRODUCTION CREDITS

First performance on 17th June 2015 at the Tabard Theatre, London.

CAST LIST

(in order of appearance)
DONALD SOWERBY – Frank Barrie
TINA - **REV. ~~THOMAS~~ HALDANE** – Philip York
CRESSIDA BRENT – Lucinda Curtis
ZOE SEYMOUR – Josie Kidd
BARRY DUMONT – John Griffiths

SETTING

The play is set in St. Augustine's Church, East London

TIME

The present

ACT 1

An afternoon in mid-June
Interval – 20 minutes

ACT 2

Scene (1) A week later
Scene (2) One year later

Director: Gareth Armstrong
Original music: Simon Slater
Lighting Design: Thomas Bezant
Assistant Director: Amy Wicks
Assistant Stage Manager: Travis Brown

CHARACTERS

Every member of the cast is well over pensionable age.

DONALD SOWERBY

Handsome, moderately successful, but aware of not fulfilling his early promise. His private and social lives are complicated by drink and an acerbic personality, which can also make him amusing company.

REV. THOMAS HALDANE

A former City broker, now vicar of a depressed East End church. Urbane and gentle, but sometimes frustrated by his work. He is intrigued by his contact with a different set of people who bring out his diplomatic and conciliatory skills.

CRESSIDA BRENT

A single woman, for whom work and an unrequited love have dominated her life. A born organiser whose bossiness cannot disguise an emotional and sometimes sentimental personality.

BARRY DUMONT

An easygoing gay man who has never let career or ambition get in the way of enjoying himself. He's astute about himself and other people and not beyond taking emotional risks in his later life.

ZOE SEYMOUR

A woman not ashamed of her past, and with no plans not to make the most of her present and future. She has no intellectual pretension and is prone to verbal howlers, but these make her a lively and engaging personality.

Scene One

The stage is in total darkness except for a red votive light down stage right. It barely illuminates a small statue. A church organ is heard, playing softly. The music fades. We could be in a confessional.

DON *(sotto)* Bless me Father… *(Pitched)* it's bloody dark in here.

TINA ~~TOM~~ Rewiring. Still can't remember where the switches are.

DON I don't carry my lighter any more. I'm on the verge of giving up.

TOM Sorry?

DON *(pitched)* I'm on the verge of giving up.

TOM Oh nil desperandum, old chap. Never give up. *(Bumps into something)* Shit!

DON Are you okay?

TOM Barked my shins.

DON There's that emergency light over there.

TOM Jesus.

DON Shins again?

TOM No the light. It's Jesus. But I don't remember a switch anywhere near Him.

TOM finds switch and illuminates a large vestry-type of room with boarded up windows, dark paint. It is full of old chairs, pews, cardboard boxes, piles of hymn books etc.

Thank goodness for that.

DON Where are we?

TOM The choir room. Well, it was the choir room when we had a choir. Now as you can see it's more of a storeroom.

DON Don't worry; it'll do for us.

TOM A bit gloomy I'm afraid.

DON Why did you cover up the windows?

TOM Couldn't afford to replace the glass. After the riots.

DON I was a choirboy you know. Rather beautiful treble. So they tell me. Is it okay if we move things about a bit? We'll put it all back when we've finished.

TOM Was he a man of faith?

DON Douglas?

TOM Yes.

DON I don't think so. If he was he didn't make a song and dance about it.

TOM You knew him a long time?

DON Getting on for ~~half a century.~~ *30 years*

TOM Were you close?

DON That's a hard one. We knew each other very well for a while.

TOM It's just that we never met, and I'd like to get a rounded view before I say my piece.

DON What piece?

TOM I always like to welcome people and speak about a life… well, a life well lived. I assume it was?

DON What?

TOM A life well lived?

DON Oh he *lived* well! He lived very well.

TOM I'm not sure that's the same thing.

DON Okay, I'll try and fill you in. Just ask away.

TOM *(gets out notebook)* I'll just jot a few things down. Family?

DON Not in the true sense of the word. Mistresses. Several.

TOM Ah. Will…any of them be here?

DON Probably not.

A very sharp tap on the door and immediately **CRESSIDA** *enters.*

CRESSIDA Oh Don! You're here before me.

DON We agreed two pm.

CRESSIDA It's exactly 1:56. You're early.

DON Sorry.

CRESSIDA I wanted to organise things.

DON Of course you did. Like what?

CRESSIDA I don't know. Put some chairs out.

DON Well, you'll be spoilt for choice here won't you? This is Reverend Haldane.

TOM Tom please.

DON This is…

CRESSIDA I'm Cressida. Hello.

TOM We were just talking about Douglas.

CRESSIDA He never mentioned you.

TOM No he wouldn't have. We never met.

CRESSIDA So what were you saying about him?

TOM I was asking about him…to get some idea of his life.

CRESSIDA Don't ask Don. You'll get a very distorted view.

DON Thank you.

CRESSIDA Well you hadn't seen him for years.

DON Why would I? In the circumstances…

CRESSIDA Oh don't bring that up now. It's hardly an appropriate time to air old grudges, and anyway it was decades ago. *years.*

TOM I'll be officiating you see, so I'd like to…

CRESSIDA Do you have to?

TOM Well it is my parish. It's customary for the vicar to welcome people, and say a few…

CRESSIDA If you must.

TOM And can you tell me, roughly, what other contributions there will be?

CRESSIDA That's why we're here.

TOM Will there be a printed order of service?

CRESSIDA It's not a funeral.

TOM I know.

CRESSIDA It's a memorial. A celebration.

DON He means the running order darling. Overture, beginners, top of the bill…

CRESSIDA Oh a programme. I hadn't that of thought.

TOM I'm happy to give you some guidance if you need it. We always use a local printer. Very reasonable. And will you need the organ? There'll be a charge I'm afraid if you want Mr. Cummings to play.

DON If we need the organ I'm sure Cressida can squeeze something out. She could find the lost chord if anyone can.

CRESSIDA Try not to be funny Don.

TOM There's a portable keyboard over there if you want to make use of it.

DON That'll be much more our style.

TOM Any idea how large the congregation will be?

DON He means the audience Cressi.

CRESSIDA Packed I hope.

TOM It's just that I've discovered that the numbers do decrease if the person to be celebrated is…over a certain age.

CRESSIDA Not for Douglas. Don't you know who he was?

TOM That's what I'm hoping to find out.

CRESSIDA (checking watch) The others are going to be late. I knew it. (She begins to rearrange chairs)

DON What sort of vicar are you, Tom? Tina

TOM Non-stipendary.

DON Is that the same as non-conformist?

TOM No, no. We're quite High here actually. It means I don't have a stipend.

DON Ah! I'm sorry. *(Beat)* What's a stipe end?

TOM It means that although I'm a vicar I don't get a commensurate salary. In brief, I don't get paid.

DON Nothing?

TOM Expenses. Some petrol allowance. Phone bill. The vicarage…

DON Ah, is it an imposing pile? Dozens of bedrooms, library, big garden?

TOM No it's a one-bedroom flat off the High Road. The vicarage was demolished years ago.

DON That doesn't seem very fair. No stipe end and no proper vicarage.

TOM Well, it's a vocation. I was called.

DON Really?/Who called you?

TOM Well… God.

DON Oh. What did he say?

TOM No, mine is a *vocation.* A calling. I was in the City you see – over thirty years, nearly forty, serving Mamon. I knew I had to do something else, something more meaningful with my life.

CRESSIDA *(banging a final chair down noisily)* I told you!

DON What did you tell us darling?

CRESSIDA They're late.

DON Only just.

CRESSIDA Still.

TOM How many are we expecting?

DON We're expecting another two.

Look, I'll slip out and see if the others are anywhere near. *(Taking out cigarettes)* Anyway, I'm desperate for a ciggy.

He goes. CRESSIDA *and* TOM *are left alone. She looks around the room disapprovingly.*

CRESSIDA   You know if you often let out this room you should think about tarting it up a bit.

TOM   I know. Since we disbanded the choir, well... I did offer it to the local Scouts but they moved in to the Adaboula Bataboulaywa Centre over the road instead. They've got wi-fi there it seems.

CRESSIDA   What do Scouts need wi-fi for? I thought it was all dib-dib with them?

TOM   It's more tweet-tweet now I think. I tried to start a Bible study group, but there weren't many takers.

CRESSIDA   Fancy. Your audience numbers going down too?

TOM   What? Oh yes. Single figures some Sundays.

CRESSIDA   I remember matinee days like that.

TOM   Ah, you're an actress then?

CRESSIDA   Good God no! Do I *look* like an actress?

TOM   Well... I suppose... I'm not sure...

CRESSIDA   Heaven forbid. No, I've got more sense. Don now, he couldn't be anything but an actor could he?

TOM   He does have a certain...

CRESSIDA   Yes, he does doesn't he.

TOM   And the other two you're expecting?

CRESSIDA   Unmistakably. You could smell them a mile off.

TOM   So Douglas was a colleague?

CRESSIDA   He was more than a colleague. He was a mentor. He was a leader. He was inspirational...he was... *(She starts to cry)* He was irreplaceable.

TOM   I'm so sorry. I didn't mean to upset you. And you were close to him, at the end?

CRESSIDA No. That's what makes this all so distressing. Until about two years ago I used to see him almost daily, and then suddenly, overnight really, he cut himself off. He found an excuse to ask for my key to his flat back, and then even stopped answering my calls. I kept thinking it was my fault, that I'd done something to upset him. He could be very moody you see…only don't put that in your "piece" will you?

TOM Of course not.

CRESSIDA Eventually I gave up trying to get in touch. The next thing I knew was a letter from his solicitors asking me to arrange this memorial. They said it was a request in his will. His will! I didn't even know he'd died. It was a horrible, horrible shock. I didn't get to his funeral. Never said goodbye.

The door opens and ZOE *and* DON *enter.*

DON Look what I found stepping elegantly from her cab!

ZOE God it's dark in here!

CRESSIDA *(recovering)* Maybe because you've still got your sunglasses on dear.

ZOE Oh what a twat I am! *(Removes dark glasses)* And do you know, the cabbie swore blind there was no such place as St. Algernon's.

TOM It's Augustine's.

ZOE What is?

TOM The church. It's St Augustine's.

ZOE What a depressing name. Algernon is much jollier.

DON He just wasn't a saint darling. Only a character in a play.

ZOE But the cabbie insisted this was the only church in the area that wasn't a carpet warehouse or a lap-dancing club.

DON You're not destined to go that way are you Tom?

TOM I fear it may only be a matter of time. *(To* ZOE*)* Hello. I'm the Reverend Tom Haldane. Tom. *Tina*

ZOE Oh *Tina* hello. Are you the recumbent vicar?

TOM The incumbent yes.

ZOE I'm Zoe. Zoe Seymour.

TOM Zoe Seymour? The Zoe Seymour? Aren't you…?

CRESSIDA And where the hell is Barry?

DON Lost?

ZOE You did check he knew the address?

CRESSIDA I sent you all the same letter.

ZOE Can we start without him?

CRESSIDA We'd only have to go back and start all over again. You know what he's like.

DON It's ages since I saw poor Barry. Bobby Baxter's wake I think it was. He looked a bit rough – you know, dandruff, and odd socks.

ZOE In what way odd?

DON No. Odd socks. Oh never mind.

ZOE Poor Barry. And he was such a handsome devil in his time. I didn't even know Bobby Baxter was dead.

CRESSIDA It was in all the papers dear. Lovely obit in The Telegraph.

ZOE Did they mention his affair with Diana Dors?

CRESSIDA Of course not. His wife's still alive.

ZOE Well *she* could hardly object. When that was going on she was finding solace elsewhere.

TOM Oh really? With whom?

CRESSIDA Zoe, do be a little discreet in front of the vicar.

TOM Tom please.

CRESSIDA In front of Tom.

ZOE *(to* TOM*)* Did you know Bobby Baxter too?

TOM No.

ZOE I thought everyone knew Bobby.

DON Not many clergymen I suspect dear.

A voice calls offstage.

BARRY Hello? Don... Cressida?

CRESSIDA That's Barry.

She opens the door and calls.

We're here dear. End of the corridor.

ZOE Try not to be too cross with the poor man.

BARRY *appears. He is immaculate in jeans, shiny brogues, and a blouson jacket.*

CRESSIDA Did you get horribly lost dear?

BARRY I wouldn't have got lost at all if you'd got the postcode right. Dmitri put it into the GPS and we ended up in a car park. Anyway the only church near where you sent us turned out to be a lap-dancing club. Dmitri had to dash off, so I put the right code into my iPhone and...voila!

CRESSIDA Who's Dmitri?

DON You've got an iPhone?

ZOE What's a GSP?

TOM GPS.

ZOE That's what I said.

TOM So you're all here then?

DON Full company.

ZOE Barry, this is the vicar, ~~Tim~~... *Tracy*

TOM Tom. Tom Haldane.

BARRY Barry. Barry Dumont.

TOM Right. Well, I'll just pop upstairs and check that the ladies doing Sunday's flowers aren't coming to blows over the chrysanths. Is there anything else you need?

CRESSIDA We'll be fine.

BARRY Don, is that your 911 GT3 outside?

DON My what?

BARRY The Porsche. Is it yours?

DON I came here on the bus. Two buses in fact.

TOM Actually it's mine.

ALL Yours?!

DON But you haven't even got a stipe end?

TOM No. But I've got a ~~pension~~ _generous payout_ from Merryl Lynch and another from Goldman Sachs. Mamon and I parted on quite good terms.

He goes.

DON Bugger me. And I was feeling sorry for him. _her_

BARRY Lovely car.

CRESSIDA What do _you_ know about cars?

BARRY They're a passion of Dmitri's. He's looking to upgrade his Lancia. He'd love that Porsche.

CRESSIDA Your friend Dmitri. Is he…?

BARRY Yes.

CRESSIDA Ah. Well, come on everyone let's get started.

They sit in an arc of chairs as laid out by CRESSIDA.

Now I've brought you each a little notebook and a pen.

ZOE How thoughtful.

DON It's just like school isn't it. And Cressida's monitor of course.

ZOE Head girl surely.

CRESSIDA Well someone's got to get things going.

BARRY Quite right C. Do you want us to write our names on the front in best writing?

CRESSIDA That'll do. Now. It looks like we'll have to let that vicar kick off. You don't suppose he'll want to say a prayer do you?

ZOE It's what vicars do darling.

DON Just think of him *her* as the warm-up man Cressi. Who's on after the reverend?

CRESSIDA I thought I should say a few words first. As I knew him the longest. Just something about Douglas's life. His achievements. His contribution to the...to the... How much he meant to us all...and how much we all...

She starts to cry.

ZOE Oh darling don't do that. You'll set us all off.

BARRY We must all try and be professional about this. It's what Douglas would have wanted.

DON *I* am being. Perfectly professional. Would you rather I did this bit? I promise I'll stay dry eyed. Throughout.

CRESSIDA I'll be alright...

ZOE ...on the night. Come on, let's all pull our socks together.

CRESSIDA Well this is what I've written so far... "Douglas Bartlett was a remarkable man, and in the 1970s was a towering figure in the world of regional theatre...

DON "Towering"? He was barely five-foot-eight.

CRESSIDA ..."From humble beginnings he went on to found the Living Laboratory Theatre in Hartlepool where we four were all privileged to work with him. His work as Artistic Director there was innovative and daring...

ZOE Daring's the word! He got me to do the first full-frontal nude scene in the whole of County Durham.

BARRY But the lighting was very discreet Zoe. Nobody could see anything.

ZOE What about that matinee when a man in the front row brought a torch?

CRESSIDA "His innovative approach to the classics and new plays attracted national attention…

DON Just a shame that Hartlepool wasn't quite ready for him.

CRESSIDA Will you let me finish! "His later career was blessed with some commercial success and I'm sure all of you here today will want to join with us, his friends and colleagues, in paying tribute to his talent, his professionalism, his zest for life, his generosity…

DON Aaaaah! Brwwwwwsh phoooom!

ZOE Whatever's the matter?

DON This is a church. That was a thunderbolt. Generous? Douglas? Did Douglas ever even buy you a drink?

ZOE Several.

DON That's because he wanted to get into your knickers. Barry?

BARRY No. But he didn't want to get into my knickers. Not that I didn't offer.

DON Cressida?

CRESSIDA I hardly drink.

DON Well that line about his "generosity" will get the first laugh of the show.

CRESSIDA "…his *generosity*". It's nothing to do with buying drinks Don. I'm talking about his generosity as an artist.

DON Aaaah. An artist.

CRESSIDA Admit it Don. You were always jealous of Douglas's success.

DON I was no such thing. Yes, he may have made a bit of money, but I thought he sold out, compromised his standards. He couldn't wait to turn his back on proper, meaningful theatre. And that play he did in the West End, remember *Don't Tell Katey*?

ZOE As a matter of fact I starred in it.

BARRY I understudied the juvenile lead.

CRESSIDA And I stage-managed it.

DON Then more fool you. It was absolute tosh.

CRESSIDA It ran for eighteen months.

ZOE I haven't been in a run like that since.

BARRY Nor me.

DON It was still tosh.

BARRY And what were you doing at the time Don?

DON I can't remember.

BARRY I can. You were playing the Button Moulder in *Peer Gynt* at Pitlochry.

DON Yes. And did you see my notices?

CRESSIDA I don't get *The Highland Gazette And Bugle*.

DON Very funny. *The Stage* said I was "immaculate".

ZOE And Barry what are the three most useless things in the world?

BARRY The Pope's balls, a nun's tits and…

ZOE/BARRY …a review in *The Stage*!

CRESSIDA Please! Not in front of you know who. We don't want any more thunderbolts.

She points at the statue above the votive light.

DON *The Guardian* said *Don't Tell Katey* "sets the English Theatre back by half a century. It is vapid, gratuitous, offensively sexist and without any discernible merit."

ZOE It still ran for eighteen months.

BARRY Do you always memorise other people's bad notices Don? Why would you do that?

DON Only the real stinkers!

CRESSIDA That's enough. We have to be out of here by four. Where was I?

DON Douglas's famous generosity of spirit…

CRESSIDA If you're going to be so negative Don, why did you agree to take part?

DON It was a three-line whip from you darling. We always jump to it for you, it's a habit of a lifetime. You said that Douglas had left money in his will for a memorial and he asked us to take part. I don't suppose he left money for a piss-up afterwards too did he?

BARRY And did he say it should be in this church?

CRESSIDA Yes. St Augustine's. God knows why, but I'm just carrying out orders here. Can I go on? "...his generosity... of spirit". Happy? Then we'll introduce ourselves. I'll go first as I'm already on my feet. *(She stands)* "I'm Cressida Brent. I had the privilege of working with Douglas for more than forty years. First as his assistant stage manager, later his stage manager and finally as his personal assistant". *(She sits)*

ZOE Me next. *(Stands)* "I'm Zoe Partridge. I was leading lady in the company where we all met more than...well, many years ago. Happy days. Later of course my career took me to the West End in leading roles, Broadway...

DON Strictly speaking off-Broadway.

CRESSIDA Shut up Don.

ZOE ...and of course countless roles on television and most importantly I suppose my role in the world's longest running radio serial, *The*–

DON It's not an audition you know Zoe.

ZOE Is that enough?

CRESSIDA It was perfect. Barry?

BARRY *(stands)* Er... Barry Dumont...

ZOE Is that your real name, "Barry Dumont"? I'd never thought to ask you before.

BARRY Well it has been for sixty-odd years so I suppose it is by now. Actually I was christened Reginald Albert Prendergast.

DON You did a wise thing then old boy all those years ago.

CRESSIDA Ignore him. Carry on Barry dear.

BARRY Actor...sometimes. Retired. I suppose.

ZOE We never *retire* darling. And you were a marvellous actor. Do you remember when we did that Pirandello play that nobody came to see? You should have been the lead darling. You were a much better actor than…er…you know…little chap, had a bald spot he used to cover up with shoe polish. Oh you know! Rumoured to have had an enormous cock.

CRESSIDA Ronald Phelps.

DON Fancy you remembering that.

CRESSIDA It was the bald spot I remembered.

DON Of course.

ZOE Ronald Phelps, of course. Well, Barry you could have acted him off any stage…out of a paper bag!

BARRY Thank you Zoe.

ZOE Not at all. And what's more you're still looking gorgeous. So smart.

BARRY Well, Dmitri chooses all my clothes; he has a very keen eye for fashion. These socks are Paul Smith.

ZOE Really? And they match perfectly, don't they Don?

CRESSIDA When you've both quite finished. Don?

DON I am DONALD SOWERBY… I am Donald Sowerby and I'm an alcoholic. I haven't had a drink for…well, since lunchtime. But it seems much longer.

CRESSIDA If you're not going to take this seriously Don we'll move on. Now we should decide what we're going to do. Readings. Poems. Songs? Did anyone come along with ideas as I asked you?

ZOE I've got a poem. Here. Ahem… *(Reads)* "Death is nothing at all. I have only slipped away to the next room. *I* am *I* and *you* are *you*…

DON Oh please! That's a bit gruesome isn't it? If Douglas is in the next room why doesn't he pop in and say hello? And of course HE is HIM and YOU are YOU…who else would you be?

ZOE There's no need to be rude. I always do it at funerals and people are very moved.

CRESSIDA It's a marvellous poem Zoe but this is meant to be a celebration. It's not a funeral. Douglas has been dead for six months.

DON So if he is waiting in the next room he'll be jolly cross by now.

ZOE Well if you don't want me to do that poem, how about some of my "St. Joan". I'm sure I can remember it. "But to shut me from the light of the sky and the sight of the fields and flowers; to chain my feet so that I can never again ride with the soldiers...

CRESSIDA Shall we keep that up our sleeves for now? It should be something that relates to our time together with Douglas.

DON That was ~~nearly half a century ago.~~ 20 years ago

BARRY But I remember it better than last week don't you? It was a marvellous time. We were always broke, always exhausted, always falling in and out of love.

DON Or falling in and out of bed in your case Barry.

CRESSIDA It had to end sometime.

DON Just a shame it had to end the way it did.

CRESSIDA Oh now's not the time Don...

DON Why not? Just because it's nearly ~~fifty~~ 30 years ago and he's dead, it doesn't mean we can forget it.

ZOE I *have* forgotten it.

BARRY And I certainly don't dwell on it.

DON I know that's what's supposed to happen when someone pops their clogs. Selective memory. You just talk about the nice bits. But what Douglas did all those years ago was rotten. It was dishonest.

CRESSIDA He was just acting on a hunch.

DON Gambling you mean.

CRESSIDA Yes, but it could have paid off.

DON It didn't. And it wasn't his money.

ZOE I suppose it was naughty of him to "borrow" some of our Arts Council Grant like that.

DON Steal is the word you're looking for! And when they got suspicious the company had to fold. He put us all out of work. Just when we were getting some real recogntion.

BARRY I *was* a bit cross when we didn't get our last three weeks' wages.

DON That was the limit. Not content with stealing public money, he takes our salaries too. And all to buy some wretched painting he'd found in a junk shop. He thought it might be a masterpiece. Well, he was wrong. Six hundred pounds for a fake French oil painting. Six hundred pounds!

ZOE It was a lovely painting though wasn't it. All those elegant ladies in their Crimplene …

CRESSIDA Crinolines Zoe. He lost every penny of his own money too remember. Even had to sell his little car.

DON Poor him! I didn't even have the train fare back to London. Had to hitchhike – from Hartlepool. No, he was quite unscrupulous. And in all these years did he ever offer to pay a penny of it back? Did you ever see your money again?

CRESSIDA Not exactly. But he did employ me for years afterwards.

ZOE And we all had that long stint with *Katey*.

DON Speak for yourselves.

BARRY But you said it was tosh?

DON He could have *asked* me.

CRESSIDA What? After you'd called him a "thieving bastard" and broken his nose?

DON He's lucky I didn't shop him to the police. They'd have put him away – embezzling funds, robbing actors.

ZOE Cressi darling whatever happened to that sweet painting?

CRESSIDA I'm not sure. I think once Douglas was told it wasn't genuine he lost interest. Probably ended up in a jumble sale. Or his attic.

DON Serve him right.

CRESSIDA Come on Don, what are *you* going to do on Wednesday?

DON Alright. Well... I usually do a bit of the Bard at memorials.

CRESSIDA But Douglas hated Shakespeare.

DON I know. "Fear no more the heat o'the sun". That's a good one. Fear no more the heat o'the sun, nor the furious winter's rages, thou thy worldly...

CRESSIDA Well, if you must.

BARRY What about you Cressi? Have you got a party piece?

CRESSIDA God no. I leave the showing off to you three. I'll just keep you all in order and make sure we don't overrun. But if you don't come up with some good ideas soon that won't be a problem. Barry you haven't offered a turn yet.

ZOE Oh you must sing something darling. As it's a church maybe you should do something a bit religious. What about the "Tia Maria". I love that.

DON I think you mean the "Ave Maria".

ZOE That's what I said.

CRESSIDA No, nothing religious. Douglas always said he's had enough of that as boy and he was a very happy atheist.

ZOE Something from a show then. Douglas loved musicals. What were his favourites?

CRESSIDA Well he hated Sondheim because he couldn't hum the tunes. For some reason he loved *The Sound of Music*.

DON In that case Barry how about "I am seventy going on eighty"?

TOM *enters carrying a picnic hamper.*

TOM I'm so sorry to interrupt but a young man just came into the church and asked me if I'd bring you this. And there's a note. It's addressed to Barry.

BARRY Oh it must be Dmitri. That's typical of the dear boy. Was he tall, blond and with a slight accent?

TOM That's him. Absolutely charming. Mrs. Arbuthnot who had her arms full of gladioli at the time nearly committed an involuntary sacrilege and spilt her vase on the altar. She was obviously rather smitten. Is he your son?

BARRY No. My husband.

TOM Ah. Well…he was…yes…erm…anyway. Absolutely charming. I'll leave this with you then.

TOM *hands over the hamper and leaves.*

ZOE That was very naughty of you Barry.

CRESSIDA Is he really…you know? Are you married?

BARRY Certainly.

DON At your age? How did you swing that? He can't have married you for your money. You've never had any.

ZOE Let's see what he's sent us. What does the note say Barry?

BARRY *(reads)* "Darling… Don't let those…" Oh just sends his love.

DON *snatches the note and reads it.*

DON Let me see. "Darling Bazzy…" Bazzy! "Don't let those old has-beens bully you…" Oh I see you've told your husband all about us then?

BARRY *(taking note back and pocketing it)* I have no secrets from him.

DON None?

ZOE Oh smoked salmon and cream cheese. May I?

BARRY Of course. I'm sure he meant us to share it.

ZOE It's very sweet of him. And Bollinger!

CRESSIDA What does Dmitri do?

DON You mean apart from drive a smart car and shop in Fortnums?

BARRY He doesn't work.

DON You're company for each other then.

BARRY He doesn't have to work.

ZOE Oh I'm intrigued. His name sounds Russian. Is he a wealthy Russian patriarch?

CRESSIDA Oligarch darling.

ZOE That's what I said.

BARRY No. But his dad is.

DON Well, are we going to just look at this bubbly?

CRESSIDA Dmitri seems to have thought of everything except the champagne glasses.

DON We could pass the bottle round. Just looking at it is making me thirsty.

ZOE Surely, the vicar chappy, Sam, must have some drinking vessels somewhere.

DON I imagine there'll be a chalice upstairs. I suppose we could pass that round like a loving cup.

CRESSIDA Come on Barry. Let's see what we can find.

BARRY Yes Cressida.

They leave.

DON You're looking marvellous darling...

ZOE For my age? Thank you Don. You know I don't think we've seen each other for a decade at least. A first night at the National wasn't it? With darling Penny being very...well, Penny. What was it? Chekov I think?

DON Ibsen.

ZOE Near enough. Oh, "An Enema For The People", wasn't that it?

DON Near enough.

ZOE I know it's very philistine Don, but I don't really get Ibsen do you? So dreary. I mean do you suppose anyone really enjoys that kind of thing?

DON Norwegians?

ZOE Well, it's been too long. *(Beat)* I thought you were off the sauce darling?

DON I was. Lasted fourteen years, two months and six days.

ZOE What went wrong?

DON Nothing went wrong. On the seventh day I decided I wanted a drink more than I wanted to stay off it. But I've got it under control this time.

ZOE Really?

DON Yes, really.

ZOE What does Fiona say?

DON Whatever she says I can't hear her. She's living in some bothy in the Highlands.

ZOE Fiona?

DON Unlikely isn't it? Do you remember Cameron Armstrong?

ZOE I think so. Did all those adverts for the Scottish Tourist Board. Rather hunky chap with red hair and a sweet little beard.

DON I always thought he looked like a ginger scrotum. But Fiona was of your mind it seems. Though now of course he looks like a grey scrotum.

ZOE Oh.

DON We'd just had enough of each other. Nobody's fault.

ZOE Yes I know, one of six and a dozen and a half of the other.

DON And you Zoe?

ZOE What about me?

DON You're...?

ZOE Fine, darling. I'm fine. Officially I'm a national treasure you know. I've just celebrated ~~thirty~~ *20* years on the programme. They were going to do a profile on me for the TV.

DON So why didn't they?

ZOE The "powers that be" thought it might disillusion the listening millions to see me in the flesh.

DON But you're still gorgeous.

ZOE Exactly. So different from my character in the programme aren't I?

DON You know Zoe darling I must confess I've never heard it. I can't bear soaps at any price.

ZOE It's not a soap Don. It's a radio drama serial. The longest running in the world.

DON I'm so sorry. So what is your character?

ZOE You really don't know?

DON Honestly.

ZOE I'm Myrtle Goldie. I run the post office. I've run the post office for…

DON Thirty years. You said/ Go on…

ZOE What?

DON Do the voice.

ZOE No.

DON Please.

ZOE No.

DON Oh please. It's such a huge part of your life and I don't know anything about it. Please.

ZOE What do you want me to say?

DON Oh… I don't know. Imagine you're talking to one of the other national treasures in the programme and…er…giving them a piece of your mind.

ZOE Very well. Let me think. Oh, I know... I'm talking to...
Mr. Hubbard the retired dairyman from Penn's Farm.

DON Go on.

ZOE *(as Myrtle in a very broad accent)* Stanley 'ubbard! If I've told
you once I've told you a thousand times not to come in
here afore wipin' them great clod hoppin' boots o'yourn on
the mat. You're old enough to know better you old varmint,
and if you think that hang-dog look is goin' to work on me
you've got another think comin'... *(Immediately and seamlessly
reverts to her own voice)* Is that enough darling?

DON No! I want you to go on. It's marvellous! No wonder you're
a national treasure. I was transfixed.

ZOE Stop it.

DON No really. And you've been doing that for ~~thirty~~ 20 years?

ZOE That's what I got my MBE for last year – servicing to
broadcasters.

DON And very well deserved. Did you get it from the Queen
herself?

ZOE No I had to make do with Princess Anne. I doubt if she's
a fan.

DON Well I am, now. I won't miss an episode from now on.

ZOE You've left it a bit late Don.

DON Why? Wouldn't I be able to follow the plot?

ZOE It's not that. It's because...no, it doesn't matter. Mmm
these olives are delicious. Try one.

DON What darling? Tell me.

ZOE No, no.

DON Tell me.

ZOE You promise you won't tell any of the others? I'm not
supposed to breathe a word. I even signed a bit of paper.

DON Cross my heart.

ZOE My days are numbered. They're writing me out.

DON My God!

ZOE There's a new editor. Just a chit of a girl. She thinks it's more important to reflect the realities of rural life than give the listeners what they want, the beloved old characters. They're closing the post office and Myrtle is retiring and moving to live with her widowed sister in a Bournemouth B&B. They're writing me a goodbye speech which I'll deliver at a farewell supper in the Memorial Hall. (That's the building on the left just past the church and opposite the duck pond).

DON You poor darling.

ZOE And that's it.

DON Won't they even give you a pension?

ZOE Who? The Post Office? I shouldn't think so Don, it's only make-believe you know.

DON No darling! The BBC. After all your years of faithful service.

ZOE The BB effing C? This isn't just mean old Aunty Beeb this is mean old Aunty Beeb *radio* – Cinderella radio. My train fare to the studio costs more than the fee they pay me. It's a joke.

DON And you a National Treasure MBE. If I'd known you were going to become a National Treasure MBE I might have felt a bit more inhibited…you know. All those years ago.

ZOE Oh I don't think you'd have let that stand in your way Don. You were very persistent.

DON And it paid off. They were a memorable couple of weeks at the end of that tour.

ZOE They were.

DON Especially Knutsford.

ZOE Why Knutsford especially?

DON That country pub we stayed in. With the empty stable block at the back. You remember?

ZOE Oh yes, Knutsford.

DON And then when the tour finished, you dropped me.

ZOE Yes.

DON And took up where you'd left off. With Douglas. What did Douglas have that I didn't?

ZOE He was single for a start.

DON So was I!

ZOE But you were engaged to Fiona.

DON Yes. But nobody knew about us, we were so discreet. And anyway it doesn't count on tour. Everyone knows that.

ZOE And the tour was over.

DON But Douglas!?

ZOE I wouldn't expect you to see it Don darling, but Douglas was a very attractive man.

DON Ah, because he was the director and useful to you?

ZOE You'd like to think it was just that I know. But a man with ambition and a streak of ruthlessness is pretty irresistible. He made it quite plain that I was only temping. And that was fine by me.

DON I've always thought of *myself* as ambitious and a bit ruthless.

ZOE Yes sweetheart, but you need something else too.

DON What?

ZOE Well if you don't know there's no point in my telling you.

They hear **CRESSIDA**, **BARRY** *and* **TOM** *coming down the corridor.*

Now, not a word Don. About my sacking. You promise.

DON Oyster, darling, oyster.

BARRY, **CRESSIDA** *and* **TOM** *enter.*

CRESSIDA No cut crystal champagne flutes to be found I'm afraid. But Tom here came to the rescue.

TOM *(producing a little stack of plastic pots)* Yogurt pots! I borrowed them from the kindergarten downstairs. I think the little ones mix their paint in them.

ZOE Well I hope you gave them a good wash. Won't you join us Bill? Susan

TOM Tom. Delighted.

BARRY Well, I'd better get this opened then.

TOM And is this a good time to talk about the order of service? The...programme. Our printers are very reliable but we should give them a few days.

CRESSIDA We've made a start but we haven't finalised anything yet.

TOM Can we at least plan the cover then?

ZOE What do you normally put on the front?

TOM The wording is usually something like, "A thanksgiving service for the life of...name...dates..." Ideally a nice photograph too. Do you have one?

DON Oddly enough I don't carry a likeness of Douglas on my person.

CRESSIDA I do. *(Finds her bag and roots about in it)* It was taken on the first night of *Katey* so it's a bit old. Ah, here it is.

ZOE *(taking the photo)* Let me see. Oh yes, he's even smiling.

DON *(taking it from ZOE)* I'd call that more of a sneer. *(Passes the photo to BARRY)*

BARRY Unmistakably Douglas though.

BARRY *passes the photo to* **TOM** *who stares at it for a long time.*

CRESSIDA Won't that do?   Bartlet

TOM It's fine, it's fine. Was...er, was Douglas Bishop a stage name?

ZOE I don't think so.

CRESSIDA Yes, yes it was. I know his real name from doing his VAT returns. It was...

CRESSIDA/TOM Dennis Tonks.

DON Dennis Tonks! Good Lord that's even worse than yours Barry.

ZOE *(to* **TOM***)* How on earth did you know?

TOM Dennis used to worship here.

CRESSIDA/DON/ZOE/BARRY Douglas?

TOM I knew him as Dennis. And yes, every Sunday.

DON My God! Am I the only one who needs a drink?

The yogurt pots are handed round as **DON** *pops the cork and pours. Everyone is a bit stunned.*

ZOE It's your champagne Barry. You should propose a toast.

BARRY Oh yes. Well...here's to Douglas.

DON Not to mention Dennis! Cheers...

Blackout   Douglas.

ACT II
Scene One

Lights up on the choir room. It is a few days later, immediately after the memorial. TOM *enters, wearing a cassock, with* DON *who is loosening his tie and removing his jacket. They carry orders of service.*

DON In my day you weren't supposed to applaud in church.

TOM Oh almost anything goes now. I did a wedding the other day and the bride entered to the theme from *Eastenders.* I didn't think that boded too well.

DON Not a bad house though was it?

TOM Very gratifying. And if I may say so, you all did wonderfully well.

DON Thank you. I thought Barry went a bit flat halfway through "Edelweiss" but then he's really more of a hoofer than a singer.

TOM And what a treat to hear Shakespeare spoken so beautifully Don. As for Zoe! That was sheer genius to do a skit on Myrtle Goldie. Wasn't that hilarious?

DON Afraid it went over my head. I've never heard the programme you see. Can't abide soaps at any price.

TOM Really? Oh, I'm such a fan, have been for years. So were most of the congregation judging by all that laughter. I haven't let on to Zoe that I'm an avid admirer in case I embarrass her.

DON Oh you wouldn't embarrass her. She'd be very touched. Especially in the circumstances.

TOM Oh?

DON Yes. They're writing her out of the show it seems.

TOM But...but they can't. Myrtle Goldie is part of the fabric of the nation. Zoe is a...a national treasure.

DON I know. And an MBE.

TOM That's terrible. It's cultural vandalism. What are they thinking of?

DON Who knows? Broadcasting standards? Not a word though. She's very sensitive about it.

TOM Of course, of course.

DON Where have the girls got to?

TOM In the vestry. There's a mirror in there.

BARRY enters, in a beautifully-cut suit.

BARRY I've just seen Dmitri off. He's picking up the new Porsche today. He's so excited, like a little boy. And he loved the show... I mean the service.

TOM It did go splendidly didn't it? I saw one or two people shed a tear during your *Sound of Music* number Barry.

DON Obviously music lovers.

BARRY And Cressi is fighting to keep the fans from mobbing Zoe in the vestry.

TOM I'd better go and rescue them then. There's nobody as relentless as a Radio Four listener is there?

He leaves.

BARRY Do you think we did the old boy justice out there?

DON I suppose we did. Maybe more than he deserved.

BARRY Well you don't slag someone off at their own memorial do you? And anyway, isn't it time you got over that business with the fake painting and the money? It was decades ago.

DON That's easy for you to say.

BARRY Why?

DON What did *you* lose? A few weeks' wages. I lost a lot more than that.

BARRY You lost a good job. We all did. Well, we're used to that aren't we? I've spent more time out of work than in it. You've been luckier.

DON Lucky? What's luck got to do with it?

BARRY Everyone knows it's seventy per cent luck in our business.

DON Seventy per cent luck! You would think that Barry. I think it's more about taking your opportunities when you get them. I had an opportunity all those years ago and Douglas snatched it from under my nose. When he did that stunt over the picture and lost us our funding Douglas had just got the rights to a new play. A brilliant new play. Everybody had been after this script, but the writer wanted it to premier in the North East. Douglas offered me the lead. We'd have got the national press in, decent agents, big managements. It would probably have transferred.

BARRY And then they'd have replaced you with a star name. You know that's the way it always goes. Or, who knows, it might have been a big flop. Maybe you had a lucky escape?

DON Oh there's no point in trying to make you understand Barry. Bazza! Be frank, you've never taken your work very seriously have you?

BARRY Maybe not. Certainly not as seriously as you. Has it made you happy?

DON Oh shut up!

BARRY No, come on. What have you got to show for all that struggling and angst?

DON My integrity.

BARRY That must be a comfort to you. It's made you bitter Don. You never used to be bitter. Waspish, yes, but not bitter. I heard about Fiona leaving you. I'm sorry. But when did you last go to the pub? Except by yourself I mean. Who are your friends? Who do you hang out with?

DON I don't "hang out" with anybody. *(Pause)* I suppose because I'm bored by mediocre people, and I resent successful ones. Can we change the subject?

CRESSIDA *enters.*

CRESSIDA Well, I tried to extract her from those demented listeners, but I think she was rather enjoying it. We were just getting away when vicar ~~Tom~~ *Tim* arrived and added fuel to the flames. I'd no idea he was hooked on the wretched programme too. I've left them to it.

DON Let her make the most of it. It's not going to last.

CRESSIDA Oh, why not?

DON Didn't you know? They've given her the boot.

BARRY From the show?

DON Yes. Maybe her terrible accent finally got too much for them.

CRESSIDA Oh poor darling. Why didn't she tell us? How did *you* find out?

DON She confided in me. We have some history you know.

CRESSIDA Everyone knows that. It was the worst kept secret in Hartlepool. But Myrtle Goldie written out after ~~thirty years!~~ *all these years!* What'll happen to her now?

DON Off to Bournemouth she said to run a B&B.

BARRY Zoe? Run a B&B? She wouldn't know where to start.

DON Not Zoe "Bazza". Myrtle whatsername. But keep it under your hats. She's sworn to secrecy by the Beeb.

BARRY Poor love. I think she thought she had a job for life.

DON A job for life! There's never been any such thing for us has there? *(Picks up his jacket and puts it on)* And now the rest of the world is finding out what that's like too. Serves them right. I'm desperate for a smoke, 'scuse me.

DON *leaves.*

CRESSIDA And a large scotch, no doubt, in "The Bells" next door? All this drinking doesn't seem to make him any more benign.

BARRY He's a very unhappy man Cressi. Were you pleased with today?

CRESSIDA It was all I could do not to blub through the whole thing. Especially that tribute from Tom. You know I'm not all that keen on God botherers, but he did do Douglas proud didn't he? He obviously recognised that deep down Douglas was a sensitive soul, and not the, well the...

BARRY The blustering old bully some people thought him. He did a good job then.

CRESSIDA I suppose I'm just a bit hurt that it was he who got to know him so well towards the end, while I was...

BARRY He explained that it was what Douglas wanted. Once he knew how ill he was he needed to live out the rest of his life in his own way.

CRESSIDA But I could have been so much help to him.

BARRY I know, and you always were Cressi. *(Beat)* He knew you loved him.

CRESSIDA What?

BARRY Of course. Everyone knew. I think he didn't want you to have the pain of seeing him...fade away.

CRESSIDA Maybe you're right. I hope you are. *(Recovering)* I didn't see Dmitri afterwards. Did he enjoy it?

BARRY Hugely. He's gone off to pick up the new Porsche. Once he'd seen Tom's he just had to have one.

CRESSIDA He's a very spoilt young man.

BARRY Yes. He is. But not by me. Do you disapprove of him?

CRESSIDA It's none of my business.

BARRY But do you?

CRESSIDA He seems very nice. But he is very young. Young for you I mean. Aren't you frightened of being hurt?

BARRY Hurt again you mean? No, I'm not frightened of it. I've got my eyes wide open this time.

CRESSIDA I think I may have heard that before.

Get chair

BARRY Shall I tell you why this is different? *(They sit)* We met online you know.

CRESSIDA That was very daring of you.

BARRY Oh everyone does that now Cressi.

CRESSIDA Well I certainly don't.

BARRY It's never too late to try.

CRESSIDA Don't be ridiculous.

BARRY Anyway, I thought he'd put up a photograph of someone else on his profile, a model or something. People often do. But then we met up. And it turned out he's not only gorgeous but also very rich.

CRESSIDA Family money?

BARRY Yes. New family money. I don't ask where his father got his roubles, but he's very generous.

CRESSIDA And what does Daddy think of you?

BARRY Ah. Well, of course he'd rather I was a blonde aristocratic heiress of child-bearing age. Actually he's a bit of an ogre, and I'd hate to get on the wrong side of him. But he does want Dmitri to be happy, and he's glad he'll get a UK passport now he's married to me.

CRESSIDA Aren't you worried that that's maybe why he did it?

BARRY Not really. Actually I did have doubts at first, but it was nothing to do with that. After I'd known him for a few weeks I told myself it was ridiculous to think a relationship like that would work – different ages, languages, cultures. I was about to call it off, tell him it was pointless to think we were compatible. And then I heard about Todd Frensham. Did you know Todd?

CRESSIDA I don't think so.

BARRY You'd have loved him. Always in West End musicals. Usually in the chorus and understudying, but just happy to be part of that world. He was so funny, so naughty. Always gave you a huge hug when you met him, and a big noisy kiss. Didn't matter where you were – a huge hug and a noisy kiss.

Well, he had this massive stroke. I went to see him in Charing Cross. They've got a special stroke unit there. He'd lost his speech. He'd lost all movement on both sides of his body. They told me he'd probably spend the rest of his life in bed or in a wheelchair. I looked at the poor sod, and realised he'd never hug anyone ever again. And I thought, here am I, around the same age as Todd, with a chance of some happiness and I'm telling myself to be "sensible" in case it all ends in tears. Well, in the end most things end in tears don't they? For someone. And if it's me at least I'll have had some great times on the way with somebody I adore. And if it does crash about my ears and we get divorced…well, I'll be a very rich gay divorcee won't I?

The door opens and **TOM** *and* **ZOE** *enter in mid-conversation.*

TOM …well, I'm astonished. And she has such a beautiful soft voice.

CRESSIDA Who does?

TOM Dora Eccles. You know. She was married to the big landowner whose son got involved with drugs and then he hanged himself in the barn when his finances got out of control. So she took up with the…

CRESSIDA I've no idea who you're talking about.

ZOE In the programme darling. Dora Eccles is played by Sonia Forbes and I was just telling Ben here…

TOM Tom. Ting

ZOE Tino Tom of course. I was just telling Tom here what a frightening old dyke she is in real life.

BARRY That's not very discreet Zoe. You'll shatter all his er illusions.

ZOE I don't give a stuff. Where's Don? I thought *he* might have been relied on to have arranged a little drinkie for us.

CRESSIDA I think he's probably making his own arrangements in the pub next door.

TOM Oh dear. I don't think he'll be there long. It's karaoke this evening at The Bells. But as you're nearly all here I just wanted to say what a pleasure it's been spending time with you. In some ways it's helped me to understand Dennis, Douglas I mean, a little better. By the time I met him I don't think he was quite the same man you were celebrating this afternoon. From your loving anecdotes he sounded rather more volatile than the man I grew to know.

BARRY He was certainly that.

TOM But over the six months he attended here at St. Augustine's he opened up to me quite a bit. I'd like to think that by the end we became friends.

CRESSIDA I do envy you that. What did you talk about? Was he very distressed?

TOM No. Reconciled I would say, very calm given his prognosis. But that's often the way. I suppose he'd been through the "why me" angry phase and he was just looking for peace. I'm not sure if I helped him find it but I can honestly say he wasn't frightened at the end.

CRESSIDA Poor Douglas. Were you with him...?

TOM I was with him the day before. The hospice rang and told me he'd died in his sleep. They were a bit anxious actually, as they'd never got any information from him about family, next of kin and so on. I couldn't help them I'm afraid.

CRESSIDA I don't think he had any family left. Didn't he ever mention his friends? Any of us?

TOM I'm sorry, but no. In fact he never talked about his work either. I'd no idea he was in the theatre. He was very focused on sorting out his affairs you see, not leaving any loose ends. His solicitor must have been instructed to dispose of his assets, but the things he had with him at the end were just enough to fill a ~~large~~ *small* suitcase.

ZOE Oh, that's so sad. What happened to it?

TOM The suitcase? Well actually... *(He points to a jumble of chairs and cardboard boxes)* It's over there. I've got so little room in my flat that I brought it here and I was going to sort it out when I had the time. Truth to tell it rather slipped my mind. Would it be an awful imposition to ask you to look through it? After all the things in there may mean more to you than me.

CRESSIDA No, no. That's fine. We can do it.

TOM Oh thank you. I'll leave you to it then. Mrs. Arbuthnot was
in a bit of a state about today's floral arrangement near the
font. She's insisting that red and white flowers shouldn't be
put together and Miss Delanay called her a "superstitious
old cow" so I think I should diffuse the situation before it
gets violent. *(Going)* And people think you theatricals are
temperamental!

> TOM *leaves. They all look to the corner where the suitcase is
> almost obscured by chairs and cardboard boxes. They are silent.*

BARRY Well?

CRESSIDA Oh you get it Barry.

> BARRY *goes and removes the detritus around the case and picks
> it up. He puts the case down in the centre of the room and they
> move chairs towards it and sit. Nobody offers to open it.* DON*'s
> voice loudly offstage:*

DON *(offstage)* The Bells, The Bells...!

> DON *throws open the door and enters a la Irving.*

...The Bells.

CRESSIDA I just knew he was going to do that.

DON What a terrible pub. How can anybody think with all that
noise. It was so bad I left before finishing my drink.

BARRY That bad, eh?

DON Fortunately they had an off-licence.

> He *produces a half-bottle of scotch from his jacket pocket,
> unscrews the top and takes a swig (probably not the first). He
> takes in the three sombre figures sitting around the case.*

Oh sorry. Am I disturbing a meeting of the coven?

CRESSIDA Actually Don this is rather important. So just pull up
a chair and shut up.

DON *(subdued)* Yes Cressi.

He joins them.

Why are we staring at this suitcase?

ZOE It's all that's left of Douglas.

DON You mean…you mean his ashes are in there?

CRESSIDA No. These are the possessions he left behind. Tom
brought it from the hospice. He's asked us to go through it.

DON Ah, I see. Well what are we waiting for?

ZOE It just seems a bit…

BARRY …intrusive.

DON He's dead for heaven's sake! He can't complain.

CRESSIDA You do it then.

DON Alright, I will.

> **DON** *hands the whisky bottle to* **ZOE** *who automatically helps
> herself to a swig.* **DON** *picks up the case and takes it to the
> same raised surface that the hamper was on in Act 1. He clicks
> open the case, throws back the lid and stands upstage of it like
> a salesman with his wares.*

What have we here? Ah, stripy pyjamas.

> *He holds them up.* **CRESSIDA** *suppresses a sob and is obviously
> distressed by what follows.*

ZOE But Douglas never wore pyjamas in bed!

DON Too much information Zoe. Some slippers. A pair of
shoes. Shirts, underwear, socks. Oh, a Bible. I suppose that
shouldn't come as such a surprise any more. A couple of
novels. Theatre programmes. Lots of pills…

CRESSIDA Oh stop it! Stop it! It's horrible. It's macabre. This
doesn't feel right at all.

DON Well you asked me to do it.

CRESSIDA I know I did and it was a mistake. Close it. Please.

DON Just a minute. What's this?

DON *pulls out a large cardboard pizza box.*

BARRY Well it looks like a pizza.

DON Yes, but there's an envelope attached to it. "Miss Cressida Brent".

CRESSIDA *jumps up and dashes over to snatch the envelope from* **DON**. *She tears it open, and reads aloud.*

CRESSIDA "My dear Cressi, have you forgiven me yet? Not just for shutting you out of my life, once I knew there wasn't much of it left, but for all the years I took you so much for granted. I couldn't have had a more devoted, a more loyal...Oh Douglas!

CRESSIDA *breaks down and* **ZOE** *gets up and goes over to her.*

ZOE Darling, shall I?

CRESSIDA *hands over the letter and sits, distraught.*

"...a more devoted, a more loyal friend... You stunk..." Oh God I'd forgotten how awful his writing is... "You stuck by me even after the professor seemed to have forgotten me." Who's the professor?

BARRY Try "profession" darling.

ZOE Oh that'll be it. "...Even after the profession seemed to have forgotten me. I hope you'll approve that I have left my estate, such as it is, to those theatre charlies...theatre charities...that ensure old topers like us..."

BARRY Troupers, maybe? Here, let me have a go.

BARRY *takes the letter and continues reading.*

"...ensure old troupers like us can end their lives in dignity. I often think of our early days in Hartlepool and the wonderful work we achieved there – you, Barry, Don and of course little Zoe. If I have my wish you'll have been reunited for at least one more occasion. An occasion that alas I shall miss. If you have fulfilled my wish I am eternally grateful. Dear Cressi, I have faith that you'll eventually receive this letter and the small token I send with it. With much love, Douglas."

DON He must mean the pizza. Here you are.

DON *hands the pizza box to* BARRY *who hands it to* CRESSIDA *who is still sitting, bereft. She takes it and opens it so that the lid obscures the contents.*

CRESSIDA Oh my God!

DON Not enough mozzarella?

CRESSIDA It's the painting. The little French painting.

CRESSIDA *takes it out of the box and shows it to them. It's a beautiful little oil painting a la Fragonard in an elaborate frame.*

ZOE It's even sweeter than I remember.

DON Fancy him hanging on to that, of all things.

BARRY What are you going to do with it Cressi?

CRESSIDA Treasure it of course!

Blackout

Scene Two

The choir room. One year later. TOM, *in civvies, watches* CRESSIDA *as she paces and looks nervously at her watch. She takes out her phone.*

CRESSIDA I could call them on my mobile?

TOM Not from here, the signal's non-existent. They said they'd call me on the church office phone at noon, so don't worry I'll be standing by.

CRESSIDA I was hoping we'd know before the others arrived.

TOM Can't be helped.

CRESSIDA You're so placid Tom. [*Tina*] Is that all part of being a vicar?

TOM Pretending to be placid certainly is. When I was in the City I was anything but.

CRESSIDA Don't you miss the excitement, the adrenaline rush of that world?

TOM There are days when I do. But there are plenty of challenges here too you know. Before my ordination nobody told me that most of my parishioners would be batty old women. The feuding. The squabbles. The sulking. The sniping. The snitching, plotting, backstabbing. They make City traders seem like…choir boys.

CRESSIDA Maybe you should have stayed with the money men.

TOM No. No, I left the City because I couldn't bear the graft, the corruption, the pursuit of wealth for its own sake. Maybe I became a priest out of guilt, the need to atone for all those [*years*] decades of accumulating wealth and not caring how it was accumulated? I thought I could do some good here.

CRESSIDA And haven't you?

40

TOM Honestly? I don't know. If this church was a business they'd be sending in the receivers – falling numbers, falling collections, decaying assets. Just look at this place.

CRESSIDA I see what you mean.

DON *enters. He is very sharply dressed and wearing sunglasses.*

TOM Don! I'm delighted you could make it. Cressida said you had a most punishing schedule.

DON Crucifying. *(He acknowledges the Jesus statuette downstage right)* Begging your pardon. I have to be across town in an hour and a half.

CRESSIDA I'm sure that will be plenty of time. Hello darling.

They embrace.

DON But for what? You were very mysterious about it, just another of your three-line whips.

CRESSIDA *(evasive)* You're looking very well. In spite of the hangover.

DON Hangover?

CRESSIDA The shades.

DON Oh, yes. *(He takes them off)* It's difficult going anywhere nowadays. And actually Cressi, I don't have a hangover because I haven't had a drink in eight months, two weeks and four days.

CRESSIDA That's marvellous. A A?

DON Cold turkey. And an extra five or six ciggies a day. You can't do everything at once.

TOM Of course not. Congratulations. Is it because of your "schedule". What is it exactly?

DON *(miffed)* You don't have a television then?

TOM Strictly a wireless man me. Always have been.

CRESSIDA Then you don't know what you're missing. Don here has become the heartthrob of the blue rinse brigade.

Ting

DON Really? What is it you do?

CRESSIDA He's Dr. Jason Hart…

DON *MR.* Jason Hart. Senior cardiologist at St Cuthbert's.

CRESSIDA He's the star of *Heartbeat Hospital.*

DON Four point six million viewers, twice-weekly.

TOM Surely, that's a soap opera isn't it? I thought you despised soaps?

DON It's a drama series actually.

TOM I'm very pleased for you. How did you land such a super job?

DON Luck really. It's seventy per cent luck in our business you know.

CRESSIDA And he's marvellous in it. So convincing. Though I suppose strictly speaking by our age a doctor would be retired.

DON Ah, but I'm not a doctor. I'm a senior consultant. At that level *we* decide when to retire.

CRESSIDA Lucky them. Lucky you. I've never retired and I don't want to retire. I've just been retired. You know I even started doing shifts at the local charity shop just to keep me occupied. But somebody complained that I "lacked empathy" with the customers, so they sacked me. Well I'm not a bloody shop girl!

ZOE enters. She looks tanned and happy.

ZOE Here we are again! Hello darlings. Hello Ron.

TOM Tom. *Ting*

ZOE That's right. And what is it now? What's the mystery? That's what I want to know.

CRESSIDA *(evasive again)* So it's just Barry we're waiting for.

TOM Yes, Barry. Will he be bringing his charming young friend…his husband?

CRESSIDA Dmitri.

TOM Of course, Dmitri.

CRESSIDA I don't suppose any of you know, but Dmitri has become an angel.

TOM Oh. Oh, I am so, so sorry. I had no idea. That is sad. He was so young. When did he pass away?

CRESSIDA He didn't pass away. He's become an Angel. He backs West End shows, using his dad's millions. They had a first night last night and Barry had to stay up with him till the early hours waiting for the notices to come out. He said he'd get here as soon as he could. *(She looks at her watch)* Er, Tom…it's nearly twelve.

TOM What? Oh, yes of course. Will you excuse me. I…er… I just need to pop out for a little while.

TOM *leaves.*

DON I'd love to know what's going on.

ZOE Me too.

CRESSIDA You're looking radiant Zoe.

ZOE Just back from the most glorious cruise. Venice, Istanbul, all around the Cyclamen islands.

DON The Cyclades.

ZOE That's what I said. It was absolutely wonderful.

DON So the Beeb gave you a golden handshake after all?

ZOE Don't make me laugh. It's only their executives they do that for. After thirty years, all I got was an appallingly written farewell speech in the village hall, and a note from Miss Smarty Pants, the editress, thanking me for all my hard work over the years. Oh, and after my last recording day I was invited for a drink – a drink – in the hospitality room for me and the cast. Cheap wine, a cheese straw and small talk with some of the dreariest people on the planet who were all thrilled to see the back of me because it means more story lines and episodes for them.

CRESSIDA You weren't sorry to leave then?

ZOE Not sorry darling. Heartbroken. It had been my life after all. What I wasn't prepared for was the aftermath. The Beeb was inundated with protests. Someone even started a "Bring Back Myrtle" group on the interweb. I got sacks and sacks of mail. It was very touching. Best of all though was the people who came out of the woodwork. People I'd lost touch with years ago. Do you know even someone from the old Hartlepool days got in touch.

DON Who?

ZOE Guess.

CRESSIDA No idea.

ZOE Go on, have a guess?

DON Er… That red-headed girl with the thick ankles…she was convinced she could get Barry into bed, poor girl. Brenda something.

ZOE No.

DON Give us a clue. Male?

ZOE Yes.

CRESSIDA Actor?

ZOE Not a very good one – says so himself. That's why he gave it up and got a proper job. Pots of money.

CRESSIDA Handsome?

ZOE Bit short for me. And that little bald spot he filled in with shoe polish has spread all over his head now.

DON Not…?

ZOE Yes!

CRESSIDA/DON Ronald Phelps!

ZOE Yes! He read about the Myrtle fuss in the paper, got in touch, and we met for coffee. Poor chap's been a bit lonely since his wife died and out of the blue he asked me to go on this cruise with him. He was so sweet to me. And before you ask – yes. It's true. He does have the most enormous…

BARRY enters, breathless as if he has been running. He carries a mound of daily papers.

BARRY So. So. So. Sorry. I had to tear myself away from Dmitri and his dad, who were getting stuck into the vodka.

DON But it's barely noon!

BARRY They are Russian.

CRESSIDA Celebrating?

ZOE How were the papers?

BARRY Almost unanimous.

ZOE Terrific!

CRESSIDA So you can expect a nice long run then?

BARRY It'll be off in two weeks. Three at the most.

DON What?

BARRY *(peeling the newspapers off and dropping them on the floor one by one)* Two stars in the Mail, ONE in The Times, two in the Telegraph – and the Express, The Sun, and the Daily Star didn't bother.

ZOE Oh dear. Didn't anyone like it?

BARRY The Guardian.

ZOE Well then, all is not lost.

DON Nobody reads The Guardian Zoe.

ZOE A lot of actors do.

DON But not many real people – actors can't afford to go to the theatre.

ZOE Oh. You must be heartbroken Barry.

BARRY Dmitri and his dad are thrilled to bits.

CRESSIDA What?

DON But surely they'll lose a fortune?

BARRY They will. But that was the whole point. Mr. Andranovitch, Dmitri's dad, had to lose half a million quid or get into a lot of trouble back home. This way they do that practically overnight.

CRESSIDA But that can't be right. That's money laundering surely? Won't they get into terrible trouble?

BARRY Papa Andranovitch has already packed his bags, and he was sure never to put Dmitri's name on anything. I won't be sorry to see the back of the old bugger, and I'm encouraging Dmitri to take up something a bit less risky now. Like lion taming.

DON Cressi, I'm going to have to go soon. And I still don't know why I've come in the first place.

ZOE Yes, you're being very mysterious. Why did you ask to meet us here of all places. Couldn't we have done tea at Fortnum's?

BARRY What's it all about?

CRESSIDA Alright. I wanted to tell you with Tom here, but I can start without him. You'll remember it's almost a year since we were last in this room together?

BARRY Of course.

CRESSIDA And you've all been busy and getting on with things. Well, it's been rather a tough time for me. The lease ran out on my flat, and they wanted some ludicrous sum to renew. On top of that as far as work's concerned I can't get arrested. Obviously no pension to speak of. Frankly I was a bit desperate and then I remembered Tom saying how much he admired that little painting that Douglas left me.

ZOE You wanted to sell Douglas's painting to the vicar?

CRESSIDA Not exactly. I was acting on a hunch really.

DON Oh don't say that. It was one of Douglas's hunches that started the whole sorry saga.

CRESSIDA I know. But it nagged at my mind. You'll think I'm soft in the head, but it was as if Douglas had passed on his feeling about the picture to me.

BARRY But it was a fake. He had it seen by some expert in Newcastle.

DON Newcastle,eh? The fine-art capital of the world?

CRESSIDA Well, actually that's what I thought. So I got in touch with Tom and came here again with the painting. He thought it was worth a shot to have it valued again. At Christie's this time.

ZOE And?

CRESSIDA The chap there got very excited. It wasn't signed but he thought there was a possibility, just a possibility mind you, that it might be by Fragonard. Jean-Honore Fragonard.

BARRY Fragonard? Really?

ZOE Even I've heard of Fragonard.

DON That would make it worth a fortune.

CRESSIDA I know. It was being x-rayed and inspected by the top chap and they would come to a decision about it today. They're phoning us at twelve. Tom's taking the call. Now.

BARRY It's ten past.

ZOE Do you suppose that's good news or bad?

CRESSIDA Whatever it is I wanted you all to be here.

ZOE To hold your hand?

CRESSIDA Not only that. If you remember we all paid for that painting.

DON Unwittingly.

CRESSIDA Even so. It was our wages that Douglas used to buy it. So whatever it's worth, we're splitting it.

ZOE Oh darling, does that mean we might all be millionaires?

BARRY Don't jump the gun Zoe. It might be worthless.

DON I'd bet money it is.

The door opens and **TOM** *is confronted by four eager faces. He is rather taken back and stays silent.*

Well?

TOM *(pause)* It's not a Fragonard.

DON I told you.

ZOE Oh Cressie darling, I'm so sorry.

BARRY Never mind Cressie, Dmitri can buy your flat and you can live in it rent free. He'll be delighted to do that for you. It'll be an investment.

TOM But...

CRESSIDA Yes?

TOM It's a contemporary. The Christie's chap says it's almost certainly by a woman called Marguerite Gerard.

DON Who?

TOM Marguerite Gerard.

ZOE Has anybody heard of her?

BARRY Nope.

DON Never.

CRESSIDA Nor me.

TOM Neither had I, I'm ashamed to say. But she was Fragonard's sister-in-law it seems. A pupil. He said if it had been a Fragonard it would be worth around fifteen million pounds.

ZOE Good heavens!

CRESSIDA I rather wish you hadn't told us that.

TOM As it is...it's only about five to six hundred thousand!

DON Good God!

ZOE How much?

BARRY Cressie!

CRESSIDA Oh, Douglas.

DON The clever old sod.

BARRY You've changed your tune.

TOM If you're agreeable Cressida, Christie's want to put it in a French genre painting auction in a couple of months.

CRESSIDA Agreeable? Of course.

BARRY And you don't have to share it Cressie. Douglas left it to you.

ZOE That's right darling. Do you really want to split it four ways?

CRESSIDA No. *(Pause)* Five. Five ways. I'd never have known what to do without Tom. He gets a fifth.

TOM I'm overwhelmed. That's astonishingly generous of you Cressida. And do you know – I know exactly what I'm going to do with the money!

ZOE/CRESSIDA/TOM/BARRY What?

The rest of the text is underscored with a pulse that evolves into a musical crescendo.

TOM This room. This bloody room. I'm going to transform it. This drab reminder of everything that's negative and failing. I want it to become somewhere positive, somewhere life enhancing. If we knock through to the hall next door we could have the most wonderful...space. A vibrant space. A performing space maybe. Somewhere for local groups... music...drama... Starting with Cressida's money we can launch an appeal. Get sponsorship. Donations. Start fund raising. We'd need a committee of course. A steering committee to organise the project. Cressida, Zoe, maybe you could be part of that?

CRESSIDA Of course.

ZOE Ah, oh I'm not really a committee sort of person Bill. I'd have no idea how to "address the chair" or "pass a motion".

DON Zoe?

ZOE Yes?

DON Never mind.

The remaining dialogue overlaps and rises in volume as everyone gets over excited.

BARRY A gala concert? That'll raise money. Dmitri and I could get that together.

ZOE Guest appearances by TV stars. Don?

DON I'm sure I can fit that in.

BARRY And music of course. Some Sondheim. I could sing some Sondheim. How about something from *Follies*? *(He starts to hum and then sing* **"THE ROAD YOU DIDN'T TAKE"***)*

CRESSIDA You'll want flexible seating in here of course Tom. I should put a bank of seats along here, another running from this wall. *(*ZOE's cue)*...You'll need to have two fire exit doors – probably here, and here. Black-out curtains hung from this wall and here, and make sure there's a tannoy in the lavatory. You don't want to give anyone an excuse for being "off".

ZOE * Or you and I could do a duet Don? How about "I Remember It Well" from *Gigi*? *(She hums it and* **DON** *joins in. They both start to sing happily)*

CRESSIDA I'll just jot down some of the equipment we're going to need.

She finds a pad and pen to make notes and doesn't notice **TOM** *moving away from her and observing the others.*

You should use multicore cables and make sure the electricity supply is fused at twenty amps per phase, terminating in about sixty-three amp sockets. The minimum rig you'll need is seven Rank Strand Prelude 28/40s, three Old Strand Pattern 764 profiles and you can use two small floods as houselights. An 8-channel mixing desk will be big enough here and make sure you install both MD and CD players and keep two powered speakers in the grid.

As **CRESSIDA** *speaks the above* **BARRY** *is singing Sondheim,* **CRESSIDA** *and* **DON** *"I REMEMBER IT WELL". An angelic choir is added to the musical mix. Tom moves downstage and, pitching over them he looks upwards.*

TOM Well Dennis... Douglas... Just look what you've done!

The votive light under the statuette starts to flash on and off. Everyone stops and looks at it in astonishment as the angelic choir music climaxes and lights fade to blackout.

The End

SETTING AND PROPS

The setting is a neglected choir room in an inner-city church. It is a repository of broken or redundant items. The room has boarded-up windows which face the audience, and no natural light. The walls can be half-panelled in dark wood and/or painted in dull green or brown. On the walls are some religious paintings, a crucifix, a broken hymn-board and a dart board.

(If preferred there need not be a standing set as the playing area can be defined by blacks, lighting, and the positioning of furniture and props.)

There is a single entrance, upstage left, that leads to the rest of the church building.

Against the wall centre-right is a long trestle table piled with unused or damaged items; broken statuary, vessels, old Christmas decorations, boxes of hymn books, choirboy surplices, parish magazines etc. Under the table, partly hidden by cardboard boxes and old curtains, is a large leather suitcase.

As far downstage right as practicable, positioned 150cm (approx.) from the floor, is a 60cm (approx.)-high statue of Jesus with a red votive light (practical) underneath.

The rest of the room contains a dozen or so church chairs in no particular configuration, a small electric keyboard (not practical), and a square table or card table downstage left.

PROPS

ACT 1

Tom's small notebook and ballpoint pen.

Don's packet of cigarettes (not practical).

Zoe's stylish sunglasses.

Cressida's large handbag containing:
4 small notebooks.
4 click-top ballpoints.
A black-and-white photograph (approx 20cm x 10cm) in a thin protective holder of a 35ish-year-old male – Douglas Bartlett.

A medium-sized Fortnum and Mason's hamper containing:
Small tins, jars and packets of edible items.
1 bottle of Bollinger (imitation) champagne (practical).

6 empty, stackable yogurt pots.

ACT 2 (SCENE ONE)

Order of service cards for the memorial with the same photograph of Douglas Bartlett.

Don's half-bottle of whisky.

A large, battered leather suitcase, with hinges and a top that can stay upright when opened. Contents:
1 pair old-fashioned striped pyjamas.
1 pair men's slippers.
Assorted items of clothing – trousers, jumpers, shirts, boxer shorts, socks.
Half a dozen partially filled pill bottles.
Old theatre programmes from the 1960s, '70s and '80s.
Three paperback novels.
A medium-sized cardboard pizza box (approx. 40cm x 40cm).
The pizza box contains a small oil painting in imitation of a French 18th Century master in an elaborate but light frame.

1 sealed envelope addressed to Cressida Brent, containing a hand-written letter.

ACT 2 (SCENE TWO)

Don's designer sunglasses.

Barry's pile of newspapers: Daily Mail/Telegaph/Times/Express/Sun/Star/Guardian.

LIGHTING AND SOUND

LIGHTING

As the only setting is a room with no natural light, the source of illumination would be the overhead lighting found in such a location. The colours chosen should be muted but not too sombre or cold. The action begins in a blackout, until the practical switch on the rear wall is switched on. This is then a permanent state in both acts, punctuated by blackouts to indicate the end of each scene, until the final page of the script when the starkness of the lighting should begin to transform and reflect the fantasy mood of the last speeches. Bold colour or special effects, perhaps even a glitter ball, can be used to briefly suggest a world of showbiz glamour. This offers the lighting team a chance to be inventive in an otherwise undemanding plot. The practical votive light under the Jesus statue down-left is activated, as indicated in the script, after the final line, and flashes on and off until the final blackout.

SOUND

Organ music can be used as pre-show and interval music, and should have popular as well as religious themes. There are no sound effects until the final stages of the play when, as indicated in the script, an increasingly insistent pulse underscores the text and is eventually drowned out by the strains of an angelic choir.

Lightning Source UK Ltd.
Milton Keynes UK
UKHW021432160120
357072UK00008B/382/P